OXFORD

And all the stars looked down

Alan Bullard

MUSIC DEPARTMENT

OXFORD

UNIVERSITY PRESS

And all the stars looked down

Gilbert Keith Chesterton (1874–1936)

ALAN BULLARD

Duration: 2.5 mins

This carol may be transposed up a semitone into E flat minor.
First published in *The Ivy and the Holly: 14 contemporary carols* (ISBN 978–0–19–336180–5).
And all the stars looked down has been recorded by The Sixteen, conducted by Harry Christophers, on the album *Song of the Nativity* (Coro).

© Oxford University Press 2008. Originally published in *Alan Bullard Carols* (ISBN 978–0–19–336485–1). This edition offprinted 2020.

Printed in Great Britain

Ma-ry's knee, His hair was like a crown, And
Ma-ry's knee, His hair was like a crown, And
Ma-ry's knee, His hair was like a crown, And
Ma-ry's knee, His hair was like a crown, And

all the flow-ers looked up at him, And all the stars looked down.
all the flow-ers looked up at him, And all the stars looked down.
all the flow-ers looked up at him, And all the stars looked down.
all the flow-ers looked up at him, And all the stars looked down.

December 2007

OXFORD CAROLS

Oxford publishes a vast array of Christmas music to suit every occasion and choir. There are pieces and collections for services, concerts, and carol-singing; pieces for SATB, upper-voice, and unison choirs; *a cappella* carols and carols with piano or organ accompaniment; and a wealth of traditional favourites alongside new carols by leading composers. There are also over 250 orchestrations of carols from *Carols for Choirs* and other collections available for hire, including versions for brass, strings, and full orchestra. With hundreds of individual titles and an impressive range of carol anthologies, Oxford provides a rich collection of the very best in Christmas music.

Selected carol anthologies from Oxford University Press

Carols for Choirs 1-5

The Oxford Book of Flexible Carols

For Him all Stars, 15 carols for upper voices

A Merry Little Christmas, 12 popular classics for choirs

An American Christmas, 16 carols and carol arrangements from North America

An Edwardian Carol Book, 12 carols for mixed voices

Alan Bullard Carols, 10 carols for mixed voices

Bob Chilcott Carols 1, 9 carols for mixed voices

Bob Chilcott Carols 2, 10 carol arrangements for mixed voices

John Gardner Carols, 11 carols for mixed voices

John Rutter Carols, 10 carols for mixed voices

Mack Wilberg Carols, 8 carol arrangements for mixed voices

Sir David Willcocks: A Celebration in Carols, 18 carols for mixed voices

World Carols for Choirs, SATB and upper-voice editions

Christmas Spirituals for Choirs

The Ivy and the Holly, 14 contemporary carols

OXFORD
UNIVERSITY PRESS

www.oup.com

ISBN 978-0-19-336442-4

9 780193 364424